MEDITATION FOR BEGINNERS

THE ULTIMATE AND EASY GUIDE TO LEARN HOW TO BE PEACEFUL AND RELIEVE STRESS, ANXIETY, AND DEPRESSION

MICHAEL DINURI

TABLE OF CONTENTS

INTRODUCTION

I want to thank you and congratulate you for buying the book, *Meditation for Beginners.*

This book contains proven steps and strategies on how to begin using meditation in your daily life. We will discuss the health benefits of meditation as well as the increased capabilities of a relaxed mind. We will talk about how meditation increases awareness and focus and thereby results in a more peaceful life with a greater ability to deal with the stress that everyday life tends to put in our path.

Not only will we talk about what to expect when you first begin meditating, we will also give you some tips on what to avoid to make the entire process easier.

This book will provide tips for those that have little time for lengthy routines or need a fast pick-me-up in the middle of the day when a regular meditation session is not possible. Techniques will also be provided for the person that just can't seem to slow the mind down long enough for a ten-minute meditation.

Examples and advice are given to make the transition from a non-meditator to a regular daily meditator smooth and simple.

Thanks again for purchasing this book and I hope you enjoy it!

CHAPTER 1:
THE HISTORY OF
MEDITATION

It is believed that meditation has been around since man has walked the earth. Imagine a prehistoric caveman gazing into his fire and allowing himself to think of nothing more than the flickering flame before his eyes. It may not have had the name or the techniques and known health benefits that we are aware of in today's society, but the motion was still the beginning phases of what we see practiced today around the world.

Throughout history and various cultures, meditation has its base roots in religion and was used to clear a person's mind so they would be free to connect with the higher power of their choosing. Every culture has early documented history of some form of meditation and the further back in history you look, the more religious the connection becomes.

Meditation has grown over the years from a basic religious practice to a common household technique. Over the past 60 years, scientists have begun to study the health benefits that meditation has on the body as well as the mind and the soul. While there have been no solid research papers published that can prove any connection that clearly defines the exact reason that meditation works for individuals, there is much proof that it does indeed have lasting effects on the body that medications alone cannot achieve. Therefore, there is mounting evidence that a regular routine of meditation can alter a person's health both physically and mentally.

It is because of this benefit to our health that we strive to provide intelligent information about the techniques, styles, and relevant tips to you, so that we may be a part of your history to reflect back upon in the future based on our success of meditation.

CHAPTER 2:
THE BENEFITS OF
MEDITATION IN
MODERN LIFE

*Meditation brings wisdom; lack of meditation leaves
ignorance. Know well what leads you forward and what
holds you back, and choose the path that leads to wisdom.*
—Buddha

Meditation is a lifestyle and as such should become as
natural as drinking water and eating food. That does not

mean that it will not require some time and effort on your part; however, the benefits will be life altering.

In today's modern society, we are entrenched in lifestyles that deprive us from the very basic concept of solitary time—a time to be alone, with no obligations, no deadlines, no responsibilities to fulfill, and no one else to please but ourselves. To most people that would sound too self-centered or selfish and therefore we come up with excuses as to why we do not spend time on ourselves. And even when we do, we tend to feel guilty afterwards and even tend to try to make up for that time through working harder at the work we have to do in our normal everyday stressful situations.

Meditation gives us the freedom to do something strictly for ourselves because it's not only good for our mind, but it has now been proven to be good for our physical health. Scientific research has documented that regular meditation can reduce stress, depression, anxiety, moodiness, and irritability. It may also help lower blood pressure and cholesterol levels, help with the pain of chronic diseases, boost the immune system, and improve lung functions. It has been shown to increase intelligence, concentration, creativity, learning ability, reasoning ability, memory, as well as increase self-esteem, alertness, and emotional control. This has an added benefit of improving relationships both personally and professionally.

It is believed that with more research, the doctors of the future will begin to prescribe meditation as a form of therapeutic treatment for a variety of ailments.

CHAPTER 3:
HOW AND WHEN TO START AND PRACTICAL ADVICE

We all have a million reasons why we don't have time in our lives to meditate. We all know the benefits and yet we continue living our daily lives struggling with stress and discomfort because we have adapted to it in our lives and do not know what life would feel like without it. So the real question is not why are we not meditating, but rather, what are we waiting for? We find time for so many other activities in our daily life that do nothing to add value to our lives, and yet we come up with excuses to a simple exercise that could make our lives so much easier and pleasanter.

Spend a few minutes and think about how much time you have spent over the past few days with things like watching television, surfing the internet, texting friends, chatting on the telephone, or maybe just plain stressed out worrying about some life event that you're struggling with. It's a proven fact that meditation can help you focus better and feel less stress, which helps you become more productive when you go about your daily life—whether it's as a CEO to a major company or studying for college classes or anything in between. Why would you not want to invest a few minutes in yourself if you knew that you could improve the remaining hours in your day?

Meditation costs nothing other than your time. You may have seen professional instructors with fancy pillows and pretty costumes teaching classes, but that does not mean you have to invest in those items to start your own meditation program. What you need is a quiet place with no interruptions, a comfortable place to place your bottom on, comfortable clothing so you can breathe with ease, and about ten to twenty minutes. Meditation can be done in less than twenty minutes or more, depending on you and your lifestyle; however, for the ease of learning, we will discuss beginning in terms of ten to twenty minute segments so you actually give yourself a real break from the world around you and allow your body time to adjust to this new skill you are learning to master. Once you have developed a technique that works for you, you will be able to adjust it to meet your needs accordingly.

There is a debate amongst professionals as to when the best time to meditate is and, again, it has to be based on your lifestyle to make it work. However, to begin, it is recommended that you practice this new skill twice a day for maximum benefit right from the start and adjust later when you have developed good skills. With that said, it's best to start with ten to twenty minutes first thing in the morning before you face any of the stresses of the day so you can begin your day on a relaxed note, and then ten to twenty minutes at the end of your day so you can go to bed relaxed and not full of tension from the day you just lived. Yes, that's twenty to forty minutes out of your day, but those will be the best minutes of each day and well worth the effort. If that is just too much to start with, then at least start each day off with a meditation session so you can begin to feel the benefits and gain an understanding of the technique and what works for you.

When you first start, those minutes will seem like hours and you might feel guilty for wasting time. That is human nature and expected, so remind yourself of the health benefits you are seeking to achieve and stick with it. If you miss one of your sessions, do not use it as an excuse to stop, use it as an excuse to reevaluate your value to yourself. You are very important and anything you can do to improve your life is something that you should continue to do, especially since it's free, something you get to have control over, and something that you have made the choice to do and not something that is controlled by outsiders. This is your body and your life. Meditation is your chance to improve both.

It is recommended that if at all possible, you practice meditation in a sitting position versus lying down. The real reason for this is that you might become so relaxed that you fall asleep, and you will not have really achieved the true benefit of meditation. However, if for health reasons you are bedridden and cannot sit upright, do not let that stop you from practicing meditation. You may need to modify your technique so that you do not fall asleep in the process; however, meditation will still have the same health benefits no matter what position you are in at the time of utilizing this skill.

Loose clothing is also recommended because it is very hard to concentrate on your breathing or any other body part or external object if you're being pinched or poked by uncomfortable clothing. It does not matter what you wear as long as you are free to breathe and relax.

Some professionals recommend a timer and others do not. That choice would have to be up to you. Personally, it's easier to not have something ticking away either physically or even mentally reminding us that time is so important that we have to be a slave to it. If at all possible, schedule your meditation time for a time when it does not matter if you go over twenty minutes so that if you feel the need to stay in a meditative state longer, you're free to do so. There is nothing wrong with having a clock or watch close by that you check to see if twenty minutes have passed, however, there is nothing more jarring to the nerves than to be relaxed and have an alarm go off. It can undo those precious minutes' worth of relaxation in a single heartbeat.

It is never advisable to meditate when you're hungry. Your mind will want to focus on your stomach and little else. If at all possible, have a small snack if you need to meditate on an empty stomach. This will allow you to focus on what you need to focus on and not what the body is lacking. The same is true for a full stomach. If you have just eaten, odds are you will fall asleep if you become fully relaxed through the meditative process.

It goes without saying that it will be impossible to meditate if you need to use the restroom. So be sure to take care of this urgent matter just prior to your meditation exercise to ensure that you are not bothered by an urge to "go" five minutes after you start to relax. Sometimes it just happens, unplanned, and can't be helped, but being aware of this issue prior to starting usually helps in the long run and helps with your comfort level.

Of course if you ever feel pain or discomfort, please feel free to adjust your posture, your location, your lighting, or whatever it is that interferes with your ability to meditate. Meditation should never cause true physical discomfort to the point of pain. You may experience some discomfort from setting on the ground if you are not familiar with sitting this way, but that will pass after a couple of days. Also, it never hurts to have supporters that can take your children or your pets for a short period of time if they prove to be a distraction that you cannot work around.

It is a good idea to speak with your doctor if you have medical issues to seek advice about what might aid you in your meditative process. Most doctors understand the therapeutic benefits of meditation and will be an encouraging supporter on your journey in this process. And if you are experiencing any kind of physical discomfort, a doctor may be able to advise you about different postures that are more suited to your body's mobility and flexibility range.

CHAPTER 4: STEPS TO HELP YOU BEFORE YOU BEGIN MEDITATING

Like any other new process in your life, you will run into obstacles, especially in the beginning. Whether it's a struggle to fit it into your daily routine or finding the method that works for you or even finding the best location that allows you to reach a fully therapeutic meditative depth, you will discover that you can easily make adjustments to your routine if you give it time to work. All habits need time to develop and meditation is no exception. You will not become a meditation master overnight no matter how enticing that may sound.

To make it easier to develop this healthy habit, there are several steps you can take to bridge the gap between your stressful life and the relaxed state you are hoping to reach. Although we will not go into great depth in any one area, we will give you a general overview of a few tricks that you might try.

The most basic is to do gentle body stretches to loosen up your muscles, which sends a signal from your brain to your body that you are about to begin some process. Over time, your mind and body will recognize this as the beginning of your meditative process.

Another easy step would be to sit quietly and take three deep breaths in a row. To do this you would inhale deeply through the mouth, hold the breath for as long as you comfortably can, and then release it slowly through your nose. This increase in oxygen has the effect of relaxing the body and helps prepare your mind and body for the meditative process to follow. This is also used as a part of some meditation processes, which we will talk about later.

There is also a method of taking a full body scan in which you slowly and methodically sit with your eyes closed and visualize each individual body part and how it is feeling as you think about it. This could be a lengthy process, however, the benefits are immense as it allows you to determine if you have discomfort that is going to affect your meditative processes and allows you to make corrections to your posture or seating arrangement prior to beginning your actual mediation.

And there are many forms of gentle exercises that can be used to get your mind into a more focused and relaxed state that have benefits of their own that will add to the benefits provided by meditation. Although we will not get into each of them, we will give you this brief list to consider:

Yoga: With the use of stretching, enhanced breath control and the strengthening of core muscles, yoga promotes mental, physical, and spiritual awareness. With its history based in India and Hinduism, it took a long time to become universally accepted. Now: *"Yoga has become a universal language of spiritual exercise in the United States, crossing many lines of religion and culture . . . Every day, millions of people practice yoga to improve their health and overall well-being . . ."* — President Barack Obama, USA

Qigong: Qigong is practiced as part of various philosophical and spiritual traditions as a means to still the mind and enter a state of consciousness that brings serenity and clarity. Many find its gentle-focused movements to be more soothing than seated meditation and it leads into a calmer sense of overall well-being prior to beginning regular seated meditation.

Pilates: A physical fitness system developed in the early 20th century by Joseph Pilates in Germany that incorporates breathing and muscle exercises that was originally called "Contrology." It encourages the mind to focus, which aids in calming the mind for the meditation process.

Tai Chi: Originally conceived as a martial arts skill, Tai Chi also has benefits in some of its forms with slow movements and monitored breathing techniques. It teaches mind and body control.

Any form of exercise or martial arts training that encourages muscle movement and breathing control is beneficial to help slow the mind down and allow you to sit still for greater periods of time. After all, that is the purpose of meditation, to allow yourself time to slow down and focus on a single purpose.

You do not have to go out and join an organization to reap these benefits, these are offered as ideas to help you solve problems with the distractions you may encounter when you first begin the meditative process. They will help, but they are by no means necessary for you to have a successful meditative process nor will they guarantee success if you are truly struggling with focus. The one thing that will help the most is your efforts to stick to the process until you figure out what it is that distracts you and then eliminate the distraction for the short period of time during your meditation sessions. You can do anything for ten minutes if you know you do not have to do it for every minute of the rest of your life. You have experience in this with everyday life in doing things that are not always comfortable, but you do them and you get through them, and you feel better once they are done. Meditation follows this same process; at first it may seem like a chore and then later on after it becomes a habit, you will wonder how you ever got through your day without this process in it.

You will struggle. Everyone does and it is up to you to determine how much value you place on your own life. If you truly want a better life, with less stress, more energy, a better outlook, and a healthier mind and body, then the beginning struggles will seem small in comparison to the gains you are going to achieve in a short time. The process of meditation is so easy that once you start, you will ask yourself why no one ever explained the process to you before so that you could have made these minor changes long ago.

Don't beat yourself up no matter how hard it is to get in the routine of meditating. You are, after all, a human being that was not raised in the environment that made meditation a normal part of life. You now have the ability to change that and to reap the benefits that have been missing from your life. You can do this and you can succeed no matter how strange or hard it seems at first. Just be patient and give it an honest try and be ready to be amazed.

CHAPTER 5:
JUST BREATHE
MEDITATION

Take a deep breath, hold it, let it out slowly. Was that hard? Probably not for most people, however, there is a proper way to do this that has maximum benefit, and some of those techniques are what we will cover in this chapter.

While we want to be in a relaxed mode, we certainly do not want to fall asleep. Some techniques have the undesirable effect of making a person extremely sleepy and we want to try and avoid that scenario.

One common form of breathing is taught frequently with yoga classes: Pranayama. Prana means "breath or life force" and yama means "control or to extend or draw out," so pranayama has been interpreted to mean "control of breath," while the exact translation is "the science of breath." The reason it is used so often in exercise routines is that it benefits the body to receive the proper flow of oxygen when and where it is needed. While there are numerous variations of pranayama based on its origins in ancient India, we will talk about two methods that are commonly used with little side effects.

The first is dirga pranayama or "the three part breath." This breathing exercise is used to calm the mind and focus the attention on the present moment. This exercise can be done while seated or while lying on your back. If done while lying on your back, you will be better able to feel your breath moving through your body as you exhale. Close your eyes and relax your body. Start by paying attention to your natural breathing without changing anything. If your mind wanders away, gently refocus your thoughts back to your breathing. Think only about how you inhale and exhale. Then inhale gently through your nose filling your belly with air until you feel rounded out. Then slowly exhale through the nose until your belly area feels empty of air and it feels like your belly button is reaching for your spine. Repeat this five more times so you have completed six cycles of deep breaths that fill and empty your belly area. On the next inhale, draw in a little more air until it feels like your ribs have moved and then slowly exhale again until you feel like there is no more air inside you. Repeat this process with the little extra air five more times for a complete cycle of six deep breaths. And now on the next inhale, draw in as much air as possible until you feel you have filled your stomach, moved your ribs, and filled your upper chest (it should feel like your shoulders are raised) and again slowly release all the air until you feel like your belly button is going to touch your spine. Continue doing this for a total of ten breaths. If at any time you become dizzy, return to your normal breathing. This exercise is about controlling your breathing and relaxing, not about causing yourself to hyperventilate and pass out. Over time, this exercise should become easier as your lungs expand and your body learns to relax into the exercise.

The second form is called sama vritti pranayama or "equal breathing" and it also helps calm the body, which leads to a more focused mind. Begin by sitting in a comfortable position and closing your eyes. Notice your natural breathing rhythms (inhaling and exhaling through your nose) but do nothing to alter it. Begin to count as you inhale. You should be about at a count of four. Now exhale so that it is at the same length of count. So if your count is four for inhale, it needs to be four for exhale. You can change the number to match your breathing style as long as you keep both numbers the same (remember, equal breathing). Maintain this breathing pattern for several minutes with your focus on your breathing, even if your mind wanders. If it does begin to wander, gently refocus your thoughts back to your breathing pattern and the count rhythm. This exercise is not only easy but very soothing.

Another Eastern breathing exercise teaches us how to breathe more efficiently (like we do when we are sleeping) to help our body make better use of the oxygen we inhale, increase our energy levels, improve our mental capacity and clarity and help us feel calmer. In this exercise, you need to lie on the floor or on a bed and once relaxed, count your normal breaths, breathing through your nose, for one minute. The average count will be between 15 and 25 breaths. Once you have that number in your mind, place a mid-sized heavy book on your lower stomach (below the belly button). Breathe in through your nose until you see the book rise. When you exhale through your nose, the book should return to its original starting place. Repeat this process for several minutes until your breathing feels natural. You may find that over time, your rate of breaths decrease to around 5 to 10 breaths per minute. These breaths will be deeper and more efficient causing more oxygen to enter the blood stream and therefore causing a soothing effect.

A point to note about breathing: cold air restricts our lungs' capacity and the ability of our lungs to transfer oxygen to our blood stream. Therefore, if you are breathing cold air, it is better to breathe through your nose to allow the air a chance to warm up prior to entering your lungs. If you are practicing breathing or meditation outdoors in a cold setting and cannot breathe through your nose, a scarf over your mouth and nose will be of benefit.

There are numerous other forms of breathing techniques that are taught in various settings around the world. If one of the methods above do not work for you, there are many more to choose from. Please be aware that some breathing methods come with a warning for people who experience hypertension or have breathing difficulties brought on by asthma or COPD. As we have stated before, if you have any medical conditions, especially ones that affect your breathing, check with your doctor prior to starting any new routine to ensure you get the proper advice needed to safely allow you to follow through with this lifestyle change. There is always a chance that your doctor may know of a technique that is suited specifically to you. The technique you choose to use is not as important as your overall success in following through and sticking to a meditation program that fits your lifestyle.

CHAPTER 6:
SIMPLE AND EFFECTIVE
MEDITATION
TECHNIQUES

Finally we are ready to begin the art of meditation. While there are thousands of sites on the internet that will teach you various methods of meditation, there is no need to learn them all. All you need is one that is suited to your needs and is easy to do on a daily basis. Believe it or not, if you have tried any of the prior exercises, you have already begun the meditative process and you may not have even realized it. Meditation is that simple.

Here are a few very simple meditation techniques to try:

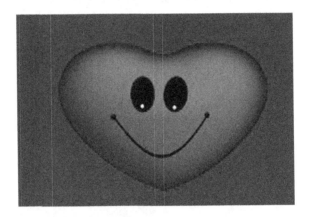

Inner Smile: Find a comfortable place to sit and relax. Close your eyes. While breathing through your nose, continue to let your body relax. Notice as your breathing becomes shallower, your face will relax. Picture your lips smiling, and let your entire body feel relaxed. Once you notice no further change in your breathing, imagine your body is smiling. Not with just your lips, but deep inside. Picture the area around or just above your stomach as a big, happy smiley face. Feel it with your body and let the smile spread throughout your body. Like the warm glow of the sunshine, let that smile fill your entire being. Bask in the warmth of that smile and know that it is a smile that is always going to be inside of you for you to connect with at any time.

You have to try this method out because words alone cannot really explain how it works. But once you have experienced it, you can reclaim the feeling at any time by simply picturing the smile inside of you. You could do this anywhere, anytime, and no one would even know you were meditating because you would not need to continually return to the initial stage of a seated position with closed eyes. Of course, it would not hurt to repeat the process daily to remind the body of how good it feels to smile on the inside. It's simple, fun, and very effective.

Natural Breathing: We touched on this one already as a warm up to meditation. It is, however, a meditation process in its own right and therefore all you would need to do is take it a step further. You would follow the steps for sama vritti pranayama or "equal breathing." Begin by sitting in a comfortable position and closing your eyes. Notice your natural breathing rhythm but do nothing to alter it. Begin to count as you inhale. The average for an adult is a count of four. Now count as you exhale so that it is at the same count as your inhale was (remember, equal breathing). Maintain this breathing pattern for the desired length of time you wish your meditation session to last with your focus on your breathing and the counting (this is the added step). If your mind wanders, gently refocus your thoughts back to your breathing pattern and the count rhythm. Before the end of your meditation session, allow your breathing to return to your natural breathing pattern and observe your natural breath. Notice how your body feels as it breathes naturally. Again, if your mind begins to wander, gently refocus your thinking back to your breathing.

Mantra: This is the version most people think of when they first hear about meditation. This is where you sit and silently, or not so silently, repeat a phrase or sound. The most common sound is "OM" (or "AUM") which is normally intoned, either silently or out loud, while exhaling. The mantra phrase should be two words (although modern mantras have been known to be an entire sentence), one used for inhales and one for exhales such as So-Ham (derived from "Ham-Sah" which is a Sanskrit phrase meaning "I am that," which means you are the very breath you breathe). When you inhale you would say "SO" (either out loud or in your mind) and as you exhale you would say "Ham" (again, out loud or in your mind). While mantra meditation was primarily a spiritual practice, it is now used as a focal point that allows us to focus our mind on something rather than allowing ourselves to become distracted by the constant chatter that occurs within our minds. Different words work well for different people due to the vibrational quality they create within our bodies. Find the word(s) from within your mind that feel right to you and stick with that choice. Also remember, once you have found a mantra that works for you, it is best to keep it to yourself and not share it with others as it may lose its ability to help you focus. Mantras produce positive energy that helps you stay focused.

Once you have decided which focusing sounds to use, find a quiet place to sit, preferably with crossed legs on the ground, with a straight back posture and close your eyes. Place your hands either palm down on your knees or with your fingers in the classic "OK" style (pointer finger touching thumbs with the remaining three fingers resting on your knees) and begin focusing on your breathing without altering it in any way. Next, begin your mantra. If the mind does try to wander, guide it back by focusing on your breathing and your mantra sound or phrase. Maintain this posture and state of mind for as long as you can, preferably ten to twenty minutes minimum, before you open your eyes. You should feel a slight vibration throughout your entire body.

As with any form of meditation, give yourself a minute or two before you transition back into the normal routine of your day. Allow yourself to sit peacefully and quietly before you rush off into the chaos that we call living. Sometimes it is best to allow yourself time for equilibrium to return after you have set for any length of time with your eyes closed. When you do rise, do so slowly as if you were swimming to the surface of awareness because, in a sense, that is exactly what you are doing. The mind needs a minute to readjust from peacefulness before it can fully engage back into all the requirements we push on it in our struggle to make it through each day. Even if you are practicing meditation in the evening, it is still a good idea to take it slowly for a few minutes after each session.

Meditation is a lifestyle change. It is best to pick a style and stay with it for an extended period of time before trying a different technique. While it may seem more exciting to mix up your routines with different versions, it can also cause distress when one method does not seem to be working. By sticking to one method, you develop the habit of meditation and get good at it before you develop excuses for why you cannot make it work for you. Especially if you're new to meditation, using several methods at once could become confusing and lead to improper techniques that would not work anyways. So find the one that sounds like a good fit and start there. Make a plan to stick with it until you have mastered it.

CHAPTER 7:
SHORT MEDITATIONS
FOR A QUICK RELIEF

Sometimes we just need a few minutes of peace and quiet. Somedays just seem like they last forever. Somedays are so filled with stress and anxiety that we wonder how we are going to have the energy to face whatever comes next. Sometimes our life is just too depressing to think about and we feel the need to get away from it all even when we know we can't. That is when it's time to grab a short meditation and get immediate relief.

Short meditations can last anywhere from one to five minutes and be done anywhere you're comfortable giving it a try. No one even needs to know what you are doing and you get to reap all the benefits to make it through some rough spots in your day.

Visualization has many techniques that can be used for this process. It's been used to combat stress, tension, and anxiety. Visualization can speed up the healing process and reduce pain and can increase the ability to focus. It's simple to use and doesn't cost anything. So let's look at a couple of these techniques.

Picture Visualization: Hang a picture that makes you sigh in a place that you can look at often. Be sure to avoid negative or depressing pictures. When you feel stressed, spend a minute or two looking at the picture while you take a few deep breaths. Do not let your mind wander to whatever is causing you stress, if it does, acknowledge the thought and return your attention to the picture. It's only a minute or two. You can do it.

Mental Visualization: Similar to the picture above, picture a place in your mind that you would rather be at. This place can be real or fictional as long as you can clearly picture it in your mind. You can close your eyes or leave them wide open depending on your ability to look within. For a few brief minutes, visit this place in your mind and do not allow yourself to think about the outside world.

The Balloon: Picture your problem in your mind, grab it, put it inside a balloon, tie it up, and release it into the wind. While it may not totally get rid of the problem in real life, it's liberating to think for a few minutes that you had control and could make it go away. It helps to make the problem regain its true perspective instead of the monster it may have started to become.

Burn it up: This trick has been used for many purposes, but it's the visual aspect that helps us release the pent up stress over any situation. Write your problem on a piece of paper, take a flame to the paper and burn it up. This is best done outdoors where you can watch the ashes blow away too. Either way, the significance of the flame is that the fire is symbolic of anger and frustration and by burning up your listed problem, the fire goes out as the problem burns up.

Then there are the breathing techniques that work well for a short break from your routine that, again, can be done anywhere without interrupting the flow of what is going on around you and without anyone knowing what you are doing. The easiest is, again, the natural breathing technique where you simply count your breaths in and out (both equal) with a metered rhythm that forces you to focus on the counting. You can do this for however long it takes to soothe your troubled spirit and regain some peace.

You could try circle breathing where you breathe in through the nose deeply, feeling the breath travel deep within, and then slowly exhale through the mouth feeling the breath rise from deep within. You focus on the feeling where the breath inside your body is traveling and how it feels entering and exiting the body. Repeat until you feel calmer.

Even lighting a candle and simply staring into the flame for a few minutes and focusing on nothing but the flicker of that flame can be used as a short form of meditation. The goal of any short meditation process is to break your mind free from the stress you are struggling with so that you can go back to the issue with a clearer mind after your break. Use whichever method works best for you to achieve this result.

CHAPTER 8: MINDFULNESS MEDITATION

Mindfulness is a practice that has been around for about 2,500 years. While it may have started officially as an aspect of Eastern religious philosophies, it is actually an act of being aware and paying attention to yourself and your surroundings. It's so natural a behavior that we take it for granted because we do it every day without thinking about it. What we fail to do is acknowledge what we are seeing and feeling most of the time.

When you add mindfulness to meditation, you add the benefit of acknowledging that you have thoughts and feelings within your mind and body and that it is okay. We don't always like our thoughts or sensations; however, they are there and it does no good to ignore them. Instead, with mindfulness meditation you open your heart and mind to accept these thoughts and sensations for what they are, without judgement, and seek a way to work through them.

Mindfulness meditation forces you to remain in the here and now and develop a better attention to the details of who you are. Meditation is not about sitting still for extended periods of time with nothing at all on your mind, because that is not how our minds work. It is estimated that the average adult mind has around 60,000 thoughts a day. That's a lot of thinking going on up there with no off switch. And we do not strive to actually turn the mind off because we truly need the brain to function continuously to keep our organs functioning properly. With meditation, we strive to focus those thoughts in a more useful manner. Mindful meditation allows us to look at some of those thoughts from a distance, acknowledge them without reacting to them, and note how they affect other parts of our body as this process occurs. Then when we step away from the meditative state, we are calmer and better equipped to handle our stressors based on factual reality instead of emotional turmoil.

There are several mindfulness meditation exercises you can try to gain a better understanding of how this works. You can do these exercises alone as a short meditation or incorporate them as part of a longer meditative session. You can do them formally or informally at any time and any place that they benefit you. Try a few out and see how you feel afterwards.

Eating Mindfully: Take a piece of your favorite food. First observe it with your eyes. Notice the color, the shape, the texture. Touch it with your finger(s). Is it hot, cold, hard, soft, or smooth? Think about the muscles in your arm and hand that are working right now. Think about what the food feels like and then pick it up and smell it. Think about the smell (or lack of smell). Listen to it. Does it make a sound of any kind when you roll it between your fingers? Now touch it to your lips. Does it feel different on your lips than it does to your fingers? Now place it into your mouth. Roll it around for a minute. Think about how it feels, tastes, interacts with your teeth and tongue. Feel your jaw muscles moving around. Go ahead and chew it. Feel how it breaks apart in your mouth before you swallow it. Close your eyes and picture it going down your throat and into your stomach.

Have you ever experienced your food in this manner before? By being mindful of the process of eating a single bite of food, you open your mind to new experiences about the actual food item. It may now taste differently than you thought it would. Try this with other types of food and see if you get similar results.

Walking Mindfully: Every day, most people walk some place at some point. Whether it's down the aisle at a grocery store, down the hallway in an office building, down your driveway, or through a park, there is a variety of opportunities to experience mindful walking. Wherever you choose to experiment with this technique, the goal is to allow yourself time to observe everything in the environment around you and how you react to it. Look at the sky. Note the color. Are there clouds? Is it bright or gloomy? How does that make you feel? Look at the surface you are walking on. Is it dirt, grass, rock, paved, or some other substance? How does it feel under your feet? Does it make a sound with each foot fall? Are you warm or cold or comfortable? Are you alone or are there other people? What noises do you hear? Are you soothed or agitated by the noises you hear? Try and observe every little detail about everything within your sight. Textures, smells, sounds, maybe even tastes or odors in the air, as they all play a part in how you will feel once you are done walking. When you are done walking, think about how different this walk was compared to the last time you walked a similar path. Being mindful causes you to heighten your awareness of the physical world around you and become more in tune with nature or the lack of nature.

Mindful Conversation: We all talk to other people every day whether it's with other adults, strangers, friends, children, family members, professionals, co-workers, or any other host of possible contacts. Most of the time we speak without a lot of forethought, which sometimes causes us stress in the long run. We have all said something at some point that we wish we could take back, but alas, the time machine has not been built yet and we are not allowed to take the proverbial foot out of our mouths. With mindful conversations we pay extra attention to body language, words that have been spoken, and allow ourselves a minute to think about our response based on what we would feel like if our response was directed at ourselves. It is a hard practice to master but well worth the effort. This mindful technique is best practiced with a friend that is willing to give you a minute to formulate your response after you have actually thought about what you are going to say (verses just blurting out whatever comes into your head like people normally do). You put yourself in the other person's position mentally to see how you would feel about your response to any statement prior to making that response. In other words, you become mindful of how other people might feel. This exercise helps you build compassion for your fellow human beings. No one wants to be the bad guy in any relationship and even close friends sometimes mess up and say the wrong thing. We are, after all, human and tend to let our emotions react for us instead of us having control of our emotions. We tend to make judgements of people without enough facts to support our belief and then instead of really listening to what that person is saying, we become distracted with trying to prove that the person is as bad as we want to believe they are. If you are using mindful conversation, you will stay focused on exactly what is being said, without adding your own judgments and creating opinions in your own mind of what you think the other person is trying to tell you. So for this exercise, you first listen intently to the other person, and after they have finished speaking (and only after) you then think about how you are going to respond in a manner that is non-judgmental, asking yourself how you would feel and what kind of a response would you want to hear. Once you have done this, you repeat the process. It is not easy. We may have two ears but we tend to talk twice as much as we listen. And our mind tends to get out of control by thinking of responses well before another person has finished speaking thereby causing us to miss the point most of the time. Mindful conversation is as much about learning to listen as it is about learning to respond.

Mindfulness can and should be practiced every day. It makes life much more enjoyable when you learn to appreciate the details of life as they occur around you on an ongoing basis. Mindfulness in meditation causes you to focus your thought processes on a single process at a time for the maximum benefit while also allowing for us to realize that the mind will continue to randomly roam to places where we wished it would not. Mindful meditation allows us to focus on this minute, right here, right now, without discounting the stress of yesterday or tomorrow. We still acknowledge the thoughts that pass through our mind, and acknowledge that emotions go with those thoughts, but we also remind ourselves that there is a time to deal with them just beyond the minutes of meditation.

CONCLUSION

Meditation allows us to take a deep breath mentally so we can a step back into reality with renewed vigor and more strength to face the challenges of everyday life. The process of meditation is simple to include into most daily routines and while it is a lifestyle, it does not require you to make major alterations to your life to begin the process.

Unlike other exercise routines, meditation does not require special equipment, expensive memberships, weekly meetings, or dietary restrictions. You get to pick the where and when and even the length of time that fits your lifestyle. You are in total control of how you want this program to work for you. Meditation is for every age and fitness level and has no religious affiliation to worry about. There is absolutely no excuse for not starting this process and successfully reaping benefits that will only improve your life now and in the future.

Thank you again for purchasing this book!

I hope this book was able to help you discover the basics of meditation and how to apply it to your life.

The next step is to begin a daily routine that includes meditation and time to reflect on your own personal value so that you may enjoy a better life with less stress, less anxiety, and a more peaceful tranquility in each day.

Finally, if you enjoyed this book, then I'd like to ask you for a favor. Would you be kind enough to leave a review for this book on Amazon? It'd be greatly appreciated!

Thank you and good luck!

Michael Dinuri
www.dinuri.com

ABOUT THE AUTHOR

Michael Dinuri is a Swedish Ayurveda, yoga, and Vaastu practitioner and author. Dinuri has always believed that life has unlimited possibilities to offer and he is passionate about helping other people change their lives and share his knowledge. As a result, he is now able to professionally work with personal development and wellness.

Dinuri's grandparents originated from northwest India, a country where yoga and alternative medicine has been used since ancient times and is still commonly used in everyday life. At an early age, encouraged and inspired by his paternal grandmother, he became intrigued by the infinite ancient knowledge and wisdom of human life and nature.

A lot of Dinuri's knowledge has been obtained through the studies of ancient scriptures and by being a disciple of well-known teachers and masters of India and other parts of the world. Dinuri also has a vast interest in mysticism and has a passion for fulfilling everyone's potential as a human being.

"The key to the road of happiness is to learn how to understand our inner being, and in doing so, be able to enjoy our every moment to the fullest."

— Michael Dinuri

OTHER BOOKS BY MICHAEL DINURI:

Ayurveda Weight Loss
Successful 10-Day Ayurvedic Detox Diet And Weight Loss Program

Lose Weight Permanently with Ayurveda and Maintain It!

The ayurvedic way of treatment can undoubtedly help in fighting against excess body fat and toxic substances. With the help of an ayurvedic detox program, the body can get rid of various health problems especially from excess fat. A 10-day ayurvedic diet program will help you get rid of excess body fat without any trouble. Using an ayurvedic way of treatment, body weight can be lost by fast and gradual ways, and thus you will not need to worry about your excess weight. Ayurveda has a complete set of solutions for every kind of weight problem you have.

Vastu Secrets in Modern Times for A Successful Life
Improve Your Health, Wealth And Relationships With Indian Feng Shui

Vastu Shastra is the art of arranging your home or work place to work in harmony with the flow of energy that surrounds us on a daily basis and to mimic nature in such a way as to honor it. Much like the Chinese art of Feng Shui, Vastu Shastra is becoming an integral part of everyday life for millions of people around the world. When we invest time in our homes and our personal well-being, there are bound to be positive effects with long reaching benefits that bring happiness and peace to our lives.

Vastu Shastra may have originated many years ago in India, however, the lessons it teaches are timeless and especially important in the current high-stress society that we live in today. Vastu wisdom teaches us to reunite with the forces of the universe to achieve personal wealth, health, and happiness on a variety of levels that can only happen once we have acknowledged and honored the endless energies that flow through our lives at any given time.

Made in the USA
Las Vegas, NV
19 July 2024